Ladies & L▮▮▮▮▮ ;

Make Great 3D Decoupage Cards

Search Press

The Publishers and author can accept no responsibility for any consequences arising from the information, advice or instructions given in this publication.

Acknowledgements

The publishers would like to thank Hayley West, who features in the photography of the step-by-step projects.

A huge thanks goes to Beth Hughes, the artist and creator of all the Jolly Nation characters.

Suppliers

If you have difficulty in obtaining any of the equipment mentioned in this book, then please visit the Search Press website for details of suppliers: www.searchpress.com

Contents

Introduction

Since their launch back in January 2006 the Jolly Nation™ 3D decoupage characters have been used to create tens of thousands of fantastic and fun cards. There are now over eighty characters in the range and we are still adding more! So why are they so popular? Maybe it is because the characters remind us of real people we all know. Maybe it is because Jolly Nation™ decoupage is so easy to use, or maybe it is just that the characters look so cute when they are created, but one thing is for sure: Jolly Nation™ is here to stay!

Making a card that is 'just right' for a close friend or relative can be a tricky task. Whether she is a niece who just adores ponies, or a best friend who is a shopaholic, you really want to show them you have made a special effort – but finding the right materials can be a problem. Well, hopefully with this book we have solved a few of those problems and added a bit of inspiration too. We have tried to make things simple by including great step by step instructions, but do not be afraid to experiment and try your own ideas. After all, getting creative is what craft is all about!

So what are you waiting for? Let's get crafting!

Materials

The following materials are needed to make the cards in this book, and they are all available from art and craft shops: white and cream card, card blanks, a craft knife and cutting mat, a pencil and ruler, large scissors, sharp scissors, 5mm (¼in) double-sided sticky foam squares, a pair of tweezers, a gold pen, an oval cutter, double-sided tape, a bone folder and photoglue.

All of these fantastic and fun cards can be made using the papers included in the back of this book.

Ballerina Girl

This project shows you how the three-dimensional decoupage builds up to make a really fantastic-looking piece, and would be ideal for any little girl – after all, how many do you know that do not love dancing?

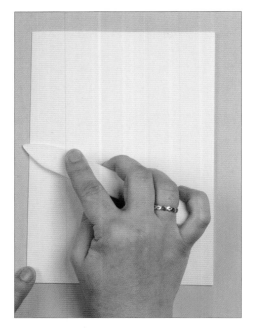

1 Fold an A4 sheet of white card in half to form a card blank. Use a bone folder to make the crease.

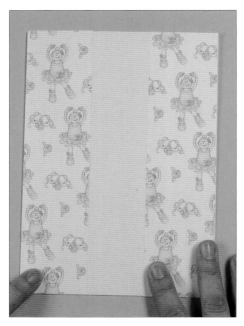

2 Cut two 5 x 21.2cm (2 x 8¼in) strips of the background paper and attach them to the card using photoglue.

3 Put the card to one side to dry. Cut out the pieces on layers 1 and 2 from the Ballerina paper.

4 Carefully attach double-sided foam pads to the backs of the pieces of layer 2, using tweezers to place them.

5 Remove the backing from the pads and carefully place the layer 2 pieces on the layer 1 piece.

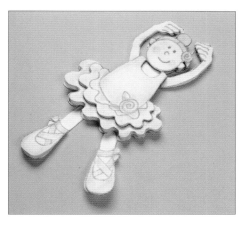

6 Repeat with the pieces from layers 3, attaching them on top on layer 2; then repeat with the pieces from layer 4.

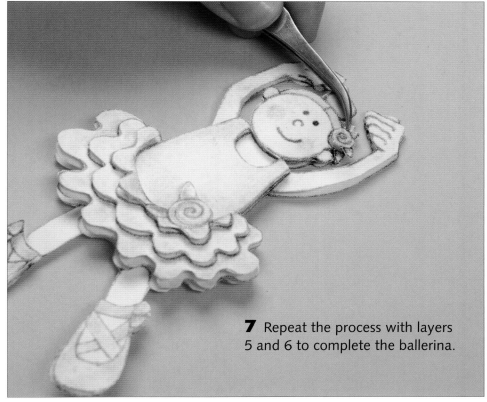

7 Repeat the process with layers 5 and 6 to complete the ballerina.

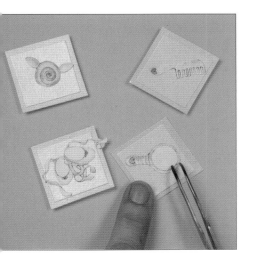

Tip
Use a craft knife and cutting mat to cut out pieces that would be awkward to reach with scissors.

8 Cut four 3.5cm (1¼in) squares from lilac card, and stick a 3cm (1in) square of pink card in the centre of each using photoglue. Cut out embellishments from the paper and stick one on to each assembled square.

9 Glue the ballerina to the centre of the card with photoglue, and mount the squares around the ballerina using foam pads.

Ponies and fairies and schooldays... One of these cards will be perfect for
the little girl in your life.

Shopping Lady

This is a slightly more complex card, but following the instructions will soon give you a very polished-looking piece. It would be great as a tongue-in-cheek card for anyone you know who enjoys the finer things in life – or perhaps just a little retail therapy!

1 Cut a piece of background paper to the same size as your card blank.

2 Run double-sided tape down the left and bottom sides of the front of the card blank, and peel the backing away partially as shown.

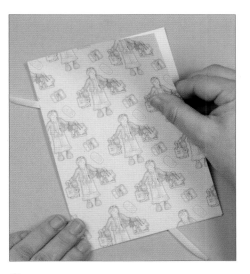

3 Place the background paper on top, securing it roughly in place with the exposed areas of tape. The tabs of backing will allow you to reposition it easily.

4 Gently pull the tabs of backing so that the paper settles in the right place, then carefully tear the background paper in a rough diagonal line from top left to bottom right.

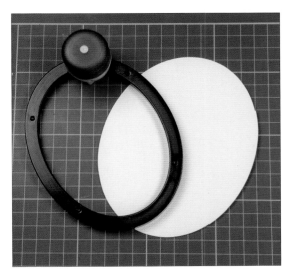

5 Use an oval cutter to cut a 14 x 11cm (5½ x 4½in) oval from cream card.

6 Run a gold pen round the edge of the oval.

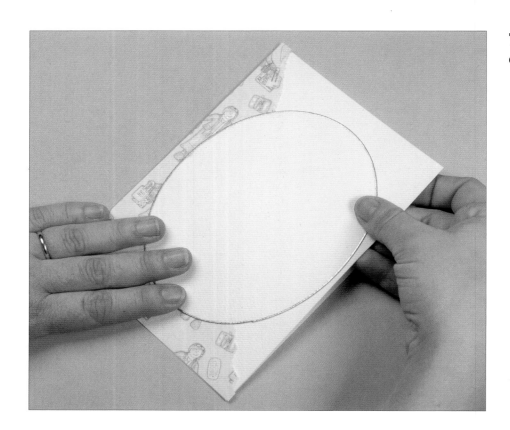

7 Use photoglue to secure the oval in the centre of the card.

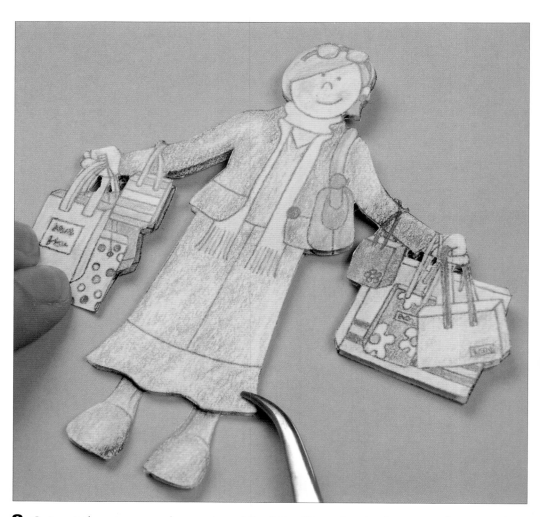

8 Cut out the pieces on layers 1 and 2 of the Shopping Lady paper, then attach layer 2 to layer 1 with double-sided foam pads.

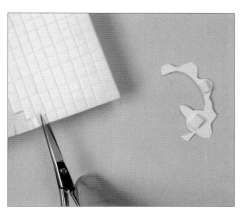

Tip
If you need to secure very small pieces, double-sided foam pads can be cut in half with sharp scissors.

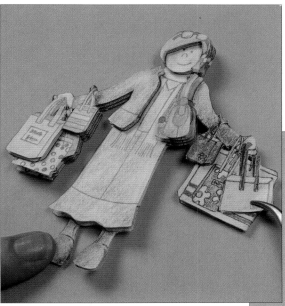

9 Repeat with layers 3 and 4 to finish the lady.

10 Use photoglue to attach the lady to the centre of the oval.

Opposite:
The finished card.

Perhaps your friends and family are more into gardening or partying than shopping, or maybe there is a new arrival in the group. Why not make a card for each of your friends?

Using the papers

Three-dimensional decoupage is the art of layering pieces of paper to give the impression of depth, and it works beautifully with these fun images to really give a bit of bounce to the finished cards. A flat picture is quickly transformed into a raised work of art, full of texture and interest – it is almost as though the character is jumping out at you!

The papers are grouped by character and background, so make sure you have the right pair once you have selected your subject.

Carefully fold and tear along the perforations near the spine of the book and remove the papers you intend to use. The numbers next to each image on the character paper show the order in which they should be mounted, starting from 1 as the bottommost layer and counting upwards.

Good luck!

3

4

5

1

2

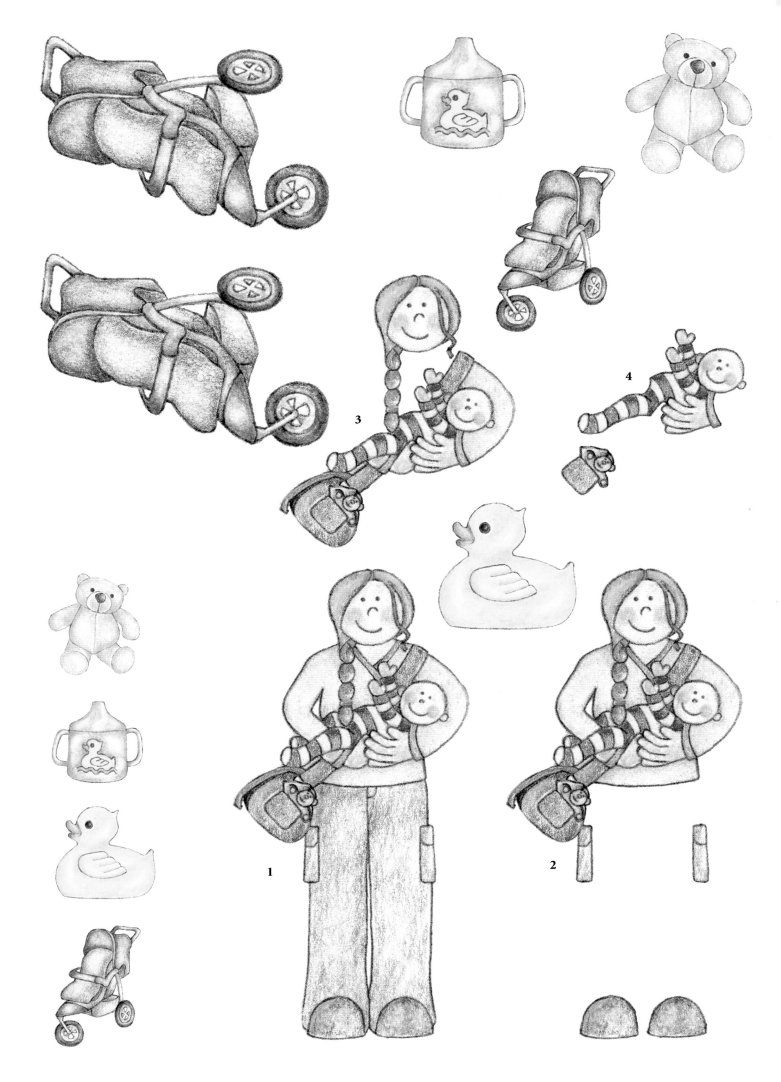

1

2

3

4

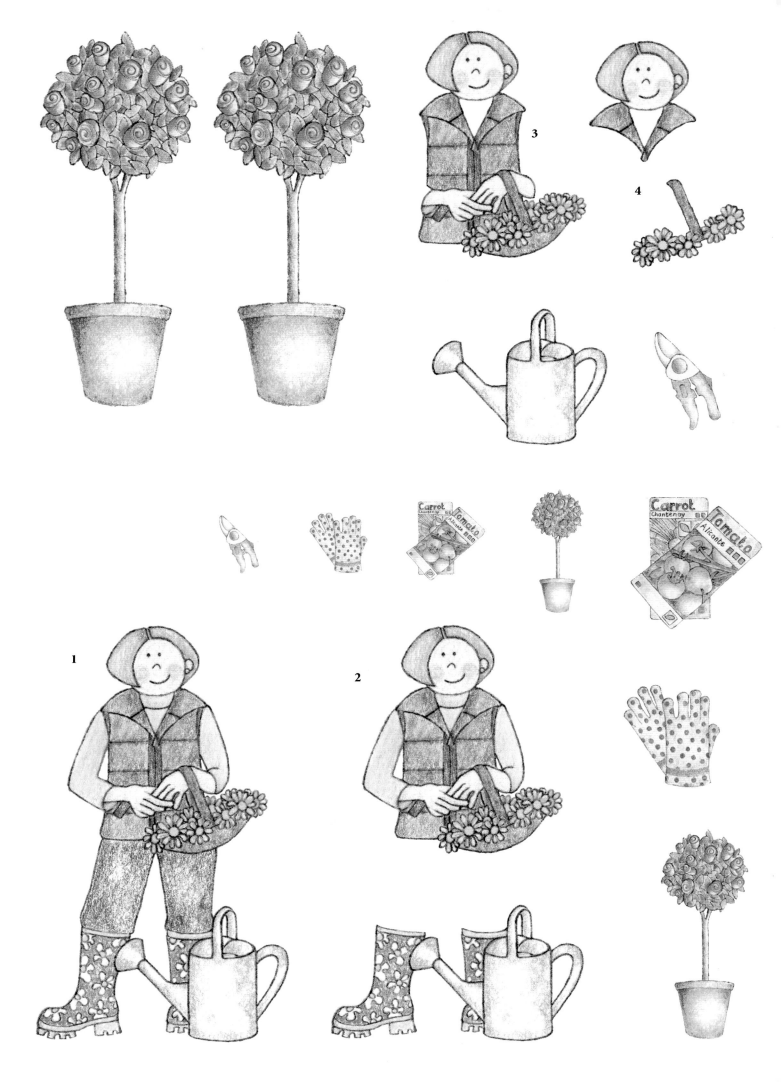

3

4

1

2

3

4

1

2